SWEDEN

EXPLORE THE COUNTRIES · EXPLORE THE COUNTRIES · EXPLORE THE COUNTRIES · EXPLORE THE COUNTRIES

Big Buddy Books
An Imprint of Abdo Publishing
www.abdopublishing.com

Julie Murray

www.abdopublishing.com

Published by Abdo Publishing, a division of ABDO, PO Box 398166, Minneapolis, Minnesota 55439.
Copyright © 2015 by Abdo Consulting Group, Inc. International copyrights reserved in all countries. No part
of this book may be reproduced in any form without written permission from the publisher. Big Buddy Books™
is a trademark and logo of Abdo Publishing.

Printed in the United States of America, North Mankato, Minnesota.
032014
092014

THIS BOOK CONTAINS
RECYCLED MATERIALS

Cover Photo: iStockphoto.
Interior Photos: ASSOCIATED PRESS (pp. 15, 16, 17, 34), Christer Fredriksson (p. 27), Getty Images
    (pp. 31, 33), Robert Gibb (p. 13), Glow Images (p. 37), iStockphoto (pp. 5, 21, 25, 29, 34, 35), Patrick
    van Katwijk/picture-alliance/dpa/AP Images (p. 19), Shutterstock (pp. 9, 11, 19, 23, 25, 35, 38).

Coordinating Series Editor: Rochelle Baltzer
Editor: Sarah Tieck
Contributing Editors: Bridget O'Brien, Marcia Zappa
Graphic Design: Adam Craven

Country population and area figures taken from the CIA World Factbook.

Library of Congress Cataloging-in-Publication Data

Murray, Julie, 1969-
 Sweden / Julie Murray.
     pages cm. -- (Explore the countries)
 ISBN 978-1-62403-347-6
 1. Sweden--Juvenile literature. I. Title.
 DL609.M87 2014
 248.5--dc23
                                          2013048636

SWEDEN

CONTENTS

Around the World

Our world has many countries. Each country has beautiful land. It has its own rich history. And, the people have their own languages and ways of life.

Sweden is a country in Europe. What do you know about Sweden? Let's learn more about this place and its story!

Did You Know?

Sweden's official language is Swedish.

Sweden is known for its beautiful forests.

PASSPORT TO SWEDEN

Sweden is located in northern Europe. Two countries border it. It is also bordered by the Baltic Sea and the Gulf of Bothnia.

Sweden's total area is 173,860 square miles (450,295 sq km). More than 9.7 million people live there.

WHERE IN THE WORLD?

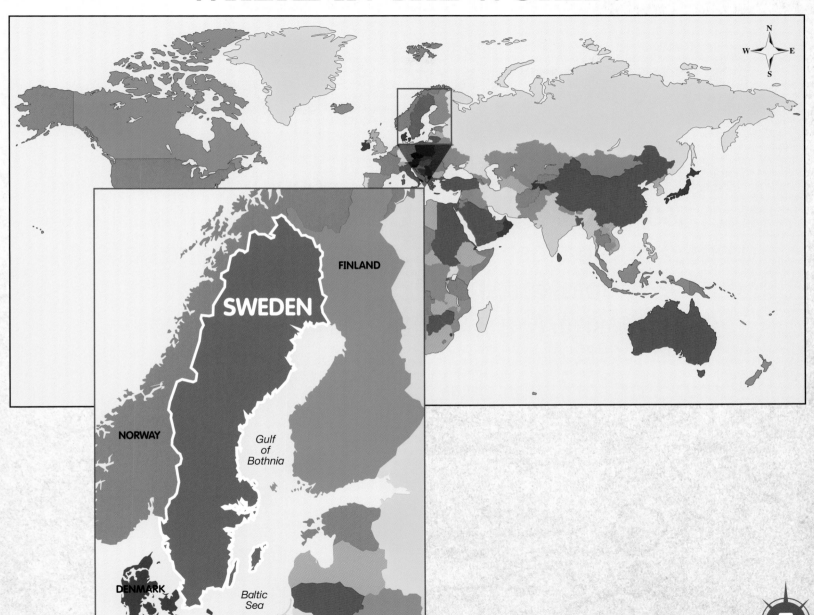

IMPORTANT CITIES

Stockholm is Sweden's **capital** and largest city. More than 860,000 people live in the city and its surrounding areas. The city is between Lake Mälaren and the Baltic Sea. It is known for its beauty.

Stockholm is Sweden's center for business. It has the country's second-largest port. One popular area is Gamla Stan, or "Old Town."

SAY IT
Stockholm
STAHK-hohlm

Stockholm is built on islands and mainland. They are connected by bridges.

SWEDEN

Stockholm

Gothenburg

Malmö

Gothenburg is Sweden's second-largest city. The city and its surrounding areas are home to more than 520,000 people. Gothenburg is Sweden's largest port. Its factories make food, cars, and cloth.

Malmö is Sweden's third-largest city. More than 300,000 people live in the city and its surrounding areas. The city is at the country's southern tip. Denmark is across the Öresund strait.

SAY IT

Gothenburg
GAH-thuhn-buhrg

Malmö
MAL-moh

Gothenburg is at the mouth of the Göta River.

The famous Öresund Link bridge connects Sweden with Denmark.

Sweden in History

Long ago, Sweden was covered by ice. As the area warmed, hunters arrived and settled the land. They hunted, gathered food, and made tools and weapons. Over time, people began to farm.

Beginning around 800, Viking tribes lived on the land. They traveled to trade goods with nearby lands. They often stole things and attacked people.

Vikings sailed in longboats.
They were powerful fighters.

Sweden became an independent country in 1523. In the 1600s, King Gustavus Adolphus helped the country grow strong. Sweden became known for its military power.

In the 1800s, life in Sweden changed as the population grew. There were not enough jobs. Around 1840, people began to leave the country to find work. By 1900, Sweden switched from mostly farming to being an **industrial** country.

Gustavus Adolphus was well educated and knew more than one language. This helped him be a strong leader at a young age.

Timeline

1436

Stockholm became Sweden's **capital**.

1901

The first Nobel Prizes were awarded. These were named for Swedish inventor Alfred Nobel.

1842

The government made elementary school required. This changed life in Sweden. As more people became educated, they had new ideas about how the country should run.

1939

As World War II began, Sweden said it would not choose a side. This war was fought in Europe, Asia, and Africa until 1945.

1969

The Swedish music group ABBA formed. They became famous around the world. Their hit songs over the years included "Dancing Queen" and "Waterloo."

2012

Princess Estelle was born. She became second in line to the Swedish throne.

AN IMPORTANT SYMBOL

Sweden's flag was adopted in 1906. It is blue, with a yellow **Scandinavian** cross.

Sweden's government is a **constitutional monarchy**. A group called the Riksdag makes laws. The prime minister is the head of government. The king or queen of Sweden is the head of state.

The Scandinavian cross on Sweden's flag stands for Christianity.

Carl XVI Gustaf became Sweden's king in 1973.

ACROSS THE LAND

Sweden is known for its beautiful land. There are mountains, coasts, **glaciers**, and forests. The country's highest mountain is Mount Kebnekaise. It stands 6,926 feet (2,111 m) high.

Sweden has many lakes and rivers. The largest lake is Lake Vänern. It is 2,156 square miles (5,584 sq km). The country's islands include Gotland and Öland.

Did You Know?

In January, Stockholm's average temperature is about 27°F (-3°C). In July, it is about 64°F (18°C).

Northern Sweden is known as "the land of the midnight sun." There, the sun does not set on certain days in the summer. That's because it is above the Arctic Circle.

Sweden's animals include brown bears, deer, fox, wolverines, and lynx. Its coastal waters, lakes, and rivers are full of fish. Salmon, herring, and cod are among them.

Thousands of different plants grow in Sweden. These include cloudberries, wildflowers, and mushrooms. Birch, spruce, and pine trees are common.

Sweden is home to reindeer.
Many live in national parks.

Earning a Living

In Sweden, most people have service jobs. Some work for the government. Others work for health care or science companies. Sweden's factories make products to sell around the world. Cars and tools are made from the country's steel.

Sweden's land and waters provide **natural resources**. Rich iron ore deposits are mined. Farmers produce beets, barley, wheat, and oats. They raise chickens, pigs, and cattle.

Did You Know?

Sweden is a leading producer of safety matches. They were invented there in 1844.

Volvo is a major carmaker in Sweden. The furniture store IKEA also got its start in Sweden.

LIFE IN SWEDEN

Sweden's people live in both the country and the city. In cities, many ride bikes to get around. They also use trains and subways.

Swedes are known to eat smörgåsbords. This is a group of hot and cold snacks. These may include cold fish, meatballs, and omelets. Cloudberries are a favorite dessert.

SAY IT
smörgåsbord
SMAWR-guhs-bawrd

Smörgåsbords are placed on a table. People can choose the foods they want.

Did You Know?

In Sweden, children must attend school from ages 7 to 16.

Swedes enjoy hockey and tennis. People also hunt, fish, bike, camp, sail, and swim. Many take part in the Vasaloppet. This is a popular cross-country ski race held in Dalarna each year.

Religion is important in Sweden. Most people are **Lutheran**.

Swedes honor Saint Lucia Day on December 13. Girls wear white clothes and a crown of leaves. One girl dresses as Lucia. She wears a crown of candles.

FAMOUS FACES

One of Sweden's most well-known people was Gustavus Adolphus. Gustavus was born on December 9, 1594, in Stockholm. Some people say he was Sweden's greatest king.

Gustavus was only 16 when he became king in 1611. He was a **Protestant** and led Sweden into a war against **Catholics**. He died in 1632 during a battle. The battle was won and Sweden gained land.

Gustavus fought in many battles.
He led his troops from the front.

Alfred Nobel was born on October 21, 1833, in Stockholm. He was a scientist and businessman. He made an explosive called dynamite. Soon, companies and the military wanted it.

Nobel was also interested in writing and traveling. When he died in 1896, he left money to start Nobel Prizes. Today, these prizes are given each year to people whose work has helped the world.

Nobel also invented fake leather, silk, and jewels.

Special events are held each year to give out Nobel Prizes.

TOUR BOOK

Imagine traveling to Sweden! Here are some places you could go and things you could do.

 ## Learn

Spend time at the Swedish Music Hall of Fame in Stockholm. There, you can see ABBA The Museum and learn about the famous music group.

 ## See

Look for the northern lights. This colorful light show can sometimes be seen in the night sky of northern Sweden.

 ## Play

Visit Astrid Lindgren's World in Vimmerby. This theater and theme park has characters from Lindgren's books, such as Pippi Longstocking.

 ## Explore

Step back in time at Gamla Uppsala, or old Uppsala. See the old church and its bell tower. Gamla Uppsala also has objects from the Viking times.

 ## Dance

Celebrate Midsummer's Eve. Every June, people put up poles decorated with leaves and flowers and dance around them. This holiday is a favorite in Sweden.

A Great Country

The story of Sweden is important to our world. It is a land of thick forests and snowy mountains. It is a country with a history of Vikings and strong leaders.

The people and places that make up this country offer something special. They help make the world a more beautiful, interesting place.

The Rök Stone in southern Sweden is a famous carving. It has letters cut in the rock. Some believe it dates to the ninth century.

SWEDEN UP CLOSE

Official Name: Konungariket Sverige (Kingdom of Sweden)

Flag:

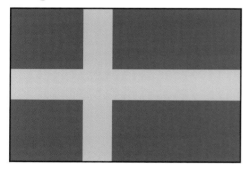

Population (rank): 9,723,809 (July 2014 est.) (91st most-populated country)

Total Area (rank): 173,860 square miles (56th largest country)

Capital: Stockholm

Official Language: Swedish

Currency: Swedish krona

Form of Government: Constitutional monarchy

National Anthem: "Du Gamla, Du Fria" (Thou Ancient, Thou Free)

Important Words

capital a city where government leaders meet.

Catholic a member of the Roman Catholic Church. This kind of Christianity has been around since the first century and is led by the pope.

constitutional monarchy (kahnt-stuh-TOO-shnuhl MAH-nuhr-kee) a form of government in which a king or queen has only those powers given by a country's laws and constitution.

glacier (GLAY-shuhr) a huge chunk of ice and snow on land.

industrial relating to the organized action of making goods and services for sale.

Lutheran a member of a Protestant church who follows the teachings of Martin Luther.

natural resources useful and valued supplies from nature.

Protestant a Christian who does not belong to the Catholic Church.

Scandinavian (skan-duh-NAY-vee-uhn) of or relating to the people, languages, or life in the countries of Sweden, Denmark, and Norway.

Websites

To learn more about Explore the Countries, visit **booklinks.abdopublishing.com**. These links are routinely monitored and updated to provide the most current information available.

INDEX